The
WARFARE
Of
FASTING

By Kenneth Scott

The Warfare of Fasting
1st Printing

ISBN: 0-9667009-7-X

To request written permission to reproduce sections of this publication, write to:

Spiritual Warfare Ministries
Attention: Kenneth Scott
P.O. Box 2024
Birmingham, Alabama 35201-2024

(205) 853-9509

Contents

Chapter 1

About Fasting

The root word that is used for "fasting" is the Greek word *nesteia*, which is a compound of *ne* (a negative prefix) and *esthio*, which means, "to eat." So the basic root meaning of the word simply means, "not to eat."

In its simplest definition, fasting is an absence of food. The word breakfast is actually composed of two words, "break" and "fast." In other words, when you eat breakfast in the morning you are breaking your fast. The average dinnertime is around 7:00 p.m. The average breakfast time is around 7:00 a.m. That means that by the time you eat breakfast, you have actually been without food for about 12 hours. So when you eat in the morning, you are breaking your fast, which is again why we call our morning meal breakfast.

There are actually two definitions for fasting. One is simply the absence of food for an unusual period of time. In other words it is considered unusual for a person to go past two meal times without eating. So if you skip any meal, you are actually fasting.

The other type of fasting is spiritual fasting. Fasting

alone will do nothing for your spirit-man. Although there are some health benefits in physical fasting, it is of no benefit to your spirit-man. Spiritual fasting on the other hand is completely different. Spiritual fasting is to go without food "not" for the purpose of health, but for the purpose of strengthening the spirit-man.

Fasting Is Still Relative

Although the purpose of fasting for physical reasons is on the rise, fasting for spiritual reasons has almost disappeared in the modern church. No one wants to fast anymore. In fact, you can listen to sermons all week long on Christian television, and yet only find one or two that will even mention fasting.

Fasting is not taught or emphasized much in our day because it has become unpopular. And unfortunately, many preachers have a tendency to stay away from preaching and teaching on subjects and issues that are unpopular for fear that it will drive members away from their church or make people think they are too radical. It has become unpopular because people don't want to do anything that will cause them to hurt, sacrifice, or make them uncomfortable.

> *That I may know him, and the power of his resurrection, and the fellowship of his sufferings...*
> *Philippians 3:10*

Everyone wants to know the Lord in the power of His resurrection. This represents walking in the miracles, signs, and wonders of the power and authority of God.

However, very few of us want to walk in the fellowship of His sufferings. Among many things, the fellowship of His sufferings represent some of the painful and uncomfortable things we must do if we want to walk in the power of His resurrection.

Jesus had to go through sufferings in order to obtain the prize. In order for a soldier to obtain victory, he must suffer the hardships of war. If we want to achieve victory in our Christian walk, we too must learn the suffering of fasting.

Many people are satisfied with the fact that Jesus died for their sins and they are going to heaven. They aren't concerned with the fact that they are living defeated lives. They have in essence accepted defeat here on earth and look forward to their ultimate rest in heaven. However, that's not the kind of life that God desires for us.

> *...I am come that they might have life, and that they might have it more abundantly.*
>
> *John 10:10*

Jesus did not come to sacrifice His life and die on the cross for us to only have eternal life; He sacrificed His life and died on the cross so that we may also be able to live a victorious life here on earth.

Although fasting may not be relative for those who are satisfied with living a defeated life, it is a necessity for those who want to live the victorious life in Christ.

The Question is Not "If" But "When"

Matthew 6:7   But <u>when ye pray</u>...

Matthew 6:16   Moreover <u>when ye fast</u>...

Fasting should be a part of every born-again believer's life. It may not be required every day, such as in the case of prayer, but it still nonetheless should be a part of your life. In the first passage above, Jesus began talking about prayer. The scripture says, *"When you pray..."* The question about prayer should not be "if" we pray, but rather, "when" we pray. Jesus taught that prayer is essential to our spiritual survival. Likewise, in the second passage, Jesus starts off the same way with fasting by saying, *"when you fast..."* Jesus was making the same point with fasting as He was making with prayer. Again, it's not a question of "if" we fast (because He is telling us that we should fast), but "when" we fast.

I have heard many people say that fasting is not essential. They say that fasting is only for church leaders. This could not be the farthest thing from the truth. While fasting is indeed for spiritual leaders, it is also for every born-again Christian. Satan will attack your life no matter who you are. So regardless of whether you are a bishop, pastor, minister, or simply a lay member, you need to fast.

In Matthew 7:24-27, Jesus gave us a parable of two houses. One of them was built upon sand, and the other was built upon rock. We all know that the main focus of the parable was about the foundation, which is the Rock of Jesus Christ. If your foundation is built upon anything else other than Jesus Christ, you are standing on shaky ground and headed for a landslide or collapse. However, the point I would like to bring out in this passage is that the same calamities came against both houses.

Being a born-again Christian does not exempt you from the attacks of the devil against your life. In fact, it amplifies his attacks against your life. Before you became a Christian, you were on the devil's side. But once you gave your life to Jesus Christ, you became an enemy against the devil, and he now wants to destroy your life. So just as prayer is necessary to fight against the attacks of the devil, fasting is not only necessary, but also essential.

Saying that fasting is not essential or necessary for our spiritual lives is like saying that proper eating, dieting, exercise, and rest is not necessary for the physical body. Although you can live a life without proper eating, dieting, exercise, and rest, this kind of lifestyle will leave you prone to stress, sickness, disease, an unhealthy body, and may even shorten your life. So yes, you can live your life without having any caution in these things, but you will have a poorer standard of life.

In the same manner, you don't really have to fast. However, just as improper eating, diet, exercise and rest can severely shorten or hamper your physical life, living your life without fasting can hinder your spiritual life and result in your being susceptible to the control and domination of Satan rather than by the Holy Spirit.

Reasons We Don't Want to Fast

To understand why it's so hard to fast, you must first understand that we are made up of spirit, soul, and body. The spirit part of you is eager to pray, fast, seek the face of God, and anything else that will draw you closer to God and give you victory in your life. However, your flesh gets absolutely nothing out of spiritual things, and therefore does not want to fast. Jesus understood this fight. He experienced it throughout His earthly life. It was prior to going to the cross that He warned His disciples with the following passage:

> *Watch and pray, that ye enter not into temptation: the spirit indeed is willing, but the flesh is weak.*
>
> *Matthew 26:41*

If you are born-again, your spirit has been awakened from death and has come alive to Christ. It is therefore willing to do whatever pleases God or draws you closer to Him. However, your flesh is weak and is vulnerable to the temptations and seductions of Satan. It is your flesh (and the cravings and desires of your flesh) that Satan uses to fight against your spirit and attempt to keep you from spiritual things. Your flesh is what Satan uses to gain control of your soul.

The soul is like a child. Unless a child is both taught and disciplined, it will be hard to get that child to do things they do not like to do. You must constantly train and discipline a child. Likewise in the spiritual realm, you must constantly train and discipline your soul if you expect to win the fight against sin, unrighteousness, and carnality. The following passage further describes what goes on in the war of the soul.

> *For the flesh lusteth [fight] against the Spirit, and the Spirit [fight] against the flesh: and these are contrary the one to the other: so that ye cannot do the things that ye would.*
>
> *Galatians 5:17*

This passage shows us that there is a constant war going on within us. Our spirit is warring against our flesh. The soul is in the middle of this war, and its control is what the spirit and flesh battles for. Fasting helps to train and discipline the soul, and thereby helps the spirit to win the fight.

The Older Shall Serve The Younger

> *And Isaac entreated the LORD for his wife, because she was barren: and the LORD was entreated of him, and Rebekah his wife conceived. And the children struggled together within her; and she said, If it be so, why am I thus? And she went to inquire of the LORD. And the LORD said unto her, Two nations are in thy womb, and two manner of people shall be separated from thy bowels; and the one people shall be stronger than the other people; <u>and the elder shall serve the younger</u>.*
>
> *Genesis 25:21-23*

Fasting is a war of the soul. Your spirit is supposed to

have dominance over your soul and flesh. In this passage, Rebecca (Isaac's wife) was pregnant with twins. She had an extremely difficult time carrying the twins and sought the face of the Lord as to why she was having such a difficult time. The Lord revealed to her that her twins represented two nations of people that would struggle against each other. The Lord also revealed to her that one nation would be stronger than the other nation, and that the elder would serve the younger.

She eventually gave birth to two sons. The name of her first son was Esau, and the name of her second son was Jacob. Esau represents the flesh, and Jacob represents the spirit. In Romans 9:13, God said, *"... Jacob have I loved, but Esau have I hated."* God was not talking about hating Esau and loving Jacob more as a person, He was talking about what they represented. Esau represents the person who is dominated, controlled and led by the lusts and desires of their flesh, while Jacob represents a person who is dominated, controlled and led by the Spirit of God. In essence, God was saying that He loves those that walk after the spirit, and He hates the sinful nature of those who walk after the lust and desires of their flesh.

In the previous passage, when the scripture says that the elder shall serve the younger, it is referring to a spiritual principle in which your flesh should be submitted and subjected to the control and directives of your spirit. As a born-again Christian, you have two birth dates. You have the day that you were born physically, and you also have the day that you were born spiritually. Our natural, physical man is much older than our spiritual man.

A person may be 35 years of age physically, but if they only gave their life and heart to the Lord 3 years ago, they are only three years old spiritually. So what God is saying is that our older man — the natural, physical man, should be subjected to the control and dominance of (the younger) our spirit-man.

Unfortunately, many Christians are controlled by Esau (their carnal mind, flesh and inert desires) rather than by Jacob (the Holy Spirit within them). Their lives are out of order and alignment according to the divine order of God. Instead of Jacob being in control, Esau is in control. Instead of the older (the flesh) serving (being subjected to) the younger (the spirit), the younger is dominated and subjected to the control of the elder. If you are led by Esau, you will sell out and compromise with the devil. And instead of your life being an arrow that points people to Christ, and a magnet that draws people to Him, it will become a hindrance that repels and keeps them away.

Fasting helps to strengthen the spirit-man, while weakening the control, strongholds and yokes of the flesh — allowing your spirit to be in control and dominate instead. Unfortunately there are many born-again Christians who (because of a lack of fasting) live defeated lives, and live in bondage to the flesh.

Many have lived their entire Christian lives experiencing spiritual defeat after defeat. It seems that they take two steps forward, and just about the time they think they have obtained victory in that area, Satan pulls them back three steps. And, because of a lifelong struggle, they eventually accept the lie from Satan that they can never have total victory in certain areas of their lives.

If Satan has told you that you cannot have victory in an area of your life, he has lied to you. He is a liar and the father of lies. If you have accepted defeat in any area of your life, you have accepted his lie. If you would begin to fast and pray about those areas you can begin experiencing victory and liberty in Christ rather than defeat.

Chapter 2

The Keys to the Kingdom

Some people who do not understand fasting would look at the title of this book, "The Warfare of Fasting," and wonder how these words "Warfare" and "Fasting" could possibly go together. It could easily be understood how warfare and prayer go together. But understanding warfare and fasting is a different thing.

The Keys to the Kingdom represent the power and authority that God has given to us and made available to us. We are in a spiritual warfare. When a person becomes born-again, God gives them weapons by which to fight, but it is up to us to utilize our weapons.

I served 13 years in the army before the Lord called me out into full-time ministry. Even though I was a combat paramedic, I spent more than half my time in the military in mechanized infantry. Some people wonder what soldiers do all day long when there is no war going on. What we did was train on our equipment. We had to train on what equipment was available to us, how to properly use it, and how to properly maintain it. Then we would go out into the field and utilize this knowledge and training in war games. After playing war games for a few weeks, we would eventually come back in and start the cycle all over again.

It was surprising to me to learn the number of soldiers that did not know how to properly use some of the basic weapons and equipment of war. There were many that did not know how to properly detonate a claymore mine, use a grenade launcher, know how to shoot and reload a machine gun, or how to properly use a rocket launcher. Sure, everyone knew how to use their personal M-16 rifle, but there was a lot more equipment available to them than their M-16 rifle. And, not knowing how to properly use some of this basic equipment in war could cost a soldier his life (as well as the lives of others around him).

It's the same way in our spiritual warfare. There are a lot of things that are available to us to overcome and defeat the enemy, but many Christians either don't know about the keys (weapons) available to them, or they are simply too (spiritually) lazy to put them in use.

> *And I will give unto thee the keys of the kingdom of heaven: and whatsoever thou shalt bind on earth shall be bound in heaven: and whatsoever thou shalt loose on earth shall be loosed in heaven*
>
> *Matthew 16:19*

Notice in the above passage, the word "keys" is plural—meaning that there is more than one key that we can use in binding and loosening the devil. I have people to call me all the time saying that they have been diligently praying for a particular thing, and it seems that their prayers are not answered. The question I have for them is this: "how many keys have you tried?" Just as there are different weapons a soldier can use to destroy his enemy on the physical battlefield, there are also different weapons (keys) we can use to destroy our enemy — the devil. You have the keys of prayer, reading and studying the Word, confession of the Word, worship and praise, and the awesome key of fasting.

Let's say that someone gave you the keys to their car and asked you to do something for them. Let's also say that they had three cars of the same make, and all their car keys looked the same. If you tried to unlock a specific car door and the key which you were using did not fit, you would then try another key, and then another until you found the one that fit.

You have to learn to do the same thing in spiritual warfare. If the key of prayer and some other key do not open the door to your deliverance, you may need to ultimately use the key of fasting. When people tell me that they have been praying and doing everything they know how to do — and still nothing avails, I always ask them if they have tried the key of fasting and prayer. When I ask this question, there are very few people that actually tell me "yes." Most of them say "no." And, the few of them that do say yes had not been faithful and diligent in their fasting and prayer.

God has given you "keys" to bind, loose, and destroy the works of Satan in your life and in the lives of others. If the key of prayer is not working for you, don't give up; use the key of fasting and prayer and unlock the door to your deliverance.

No weapon that is formed against thee shall
prosper; and every tongue that shall rise against

thee in judgment thou shalt condemn. This is the heritage of the servants of the LORD, and their righteousness is of me, saith the LORD.
Isaiah 54:17

Just about every Christian knows the above scripture passage by memory, and can even quote it verbatim. But what most Christians do not understand about this passage is that the promises of God are under a condition. The promises and blessings of God are under the conditions of our obedience to His Word.

For Example: We like to quote Deuteronomy Chapter 28 where God talks about all the blessings that shall come upon us. But the blessings of the Lord are contingent upon our obedience. Because, in the later half of the same chapter it also talks about the curses that shall come upon us if we do not obey the Word of God.

The above passage only serves to be true if you are willing to follow God's Word and use the equipment (keys to the kingdom) that is available to you. A solider cannot expect his weapons to work properly if he does not properly clean and maintain them. Likewise, if we do not properly utilize the keys to the kingdom (including fasting), then some weapons of the devil may actually prosper against us.

Fasting and Prayer

In the book of Matthew, chapter 6, beginning at verse 6, Jesus begins a teaching on prayer. This passage is better known to us as, "The Lord's Prayer." Many think He ends His teaching with verse 13. However, He actually ends His teaching on prayer with verse 18 talking about fasting.

After finishing the teaching on prayer, He continues it with two points that are key for us in prayer — forgiveness and fasting. He did not include them in the teaching outline on the Lord's Prayer simply because they may not be every day issues, as with those outlined in "The Lord's Prayer." But even though forgiveness and fasting are not things we may need to do every day, they are both key to our effectiveness in prayer.

Forgiveness is a key part of prayer because if you do not forgive others, the devil can use the anger, strife, bitterness and unforgiveness in your heart to not only hinder your prayers, but to also get a stronghold on your life. Unforgiveness stops your prayer in its tracks and opens the door for Satan and demonic activity in your life.

* Note: Please see our book on *"Understanding the Lord's Prayer"* for an in-depth understanding on this point as well as an understanding of the entire outline of the Lord's prayer and its meaning.

Fasting is a key part of prayer because together, fasting and prayer gives you the power you need to overcome the enemy, as well as his attempts to deceive, hinder, bind, or destroy you.

You can have prayer without fasting, but you cannot have fasting without prayer. There is nowhere in the Bible where you can find someone obtaining victory from fasting without combining it with prayer. When you fast and do not pray, you are only dieting. Although there are some health benefits to fasting alone, without prayer, it has no spiritual benefit.

Prayer is powerful in itself. If you were to describe prayer as a weapon in a natural war, it could be described as laser-guided bombs and missiles that destroy the enemy and his positions. But prayer along with fasting would be described as launching a laser guided nuclear bomb against the enemy—wiping out everything in its path.

When bombs are dropped on an enemy's position, it causes severe damage to their personnel, equipment, and position, but it sometimes does not destroy everything—especially if the enemy is dug in. But when you pray and fast together, it becomes like a nuclear explosion destroying everything in its path.

Chapter 3

What Happens In the Spiritual Realm When We Pray

W hen we pray, God does not sit in heaven playing games with us waiting to see how hard or long we will pray. When we pray according to the Word of God, He dispatches His angels with the answers to our prayers.

> *Ask, and it shall be given you; seek, and ye shall find; knock, and it shall be opened unto you: For every one that asketh receiveth; and he that seeketh findeth; and to him that knocketh it shall be opened. Or what man is there of you, whom if his son ask bread, will he give him a stone? Or if he ask a fish, will he give him a serpent? If ye then, being evil, know how to give good gifts unto your children, how much more shall your Father which is in heaven give good things to them that ask him?*
>
> *Matthew 7:7-11*

In this passage Jesus shows us the process of prayer. If you are a born-again child of God and you ask God for something in prayer according to His Word, God answers your prayers. In the preceding scripture passage Jesus gives us a parallel that helps us to understand God's desire and willingness to answer our prayers when we pray.

The parallel is this: Just as earthly parents who love their children would not give them anything evil or harmful when they are in need and ask them for something, God will likewise not hold back any needful thing from us, or give us something wrong or evil when we correctly ask Him in prayer.

So if this is true, then what happens to our prayers when we pray? To understand this question, let's look at the following passage:

> *Then said he unto me, Fear not, Daniel: for from the first day that thou didst set thine heart to understand, and to chasten thyself before thy God, thy words were heard, and I am come for thy words. But the prince of the kingdom of Persia withstood me one and twenty days: but, lo, Michael, one of the chief princes, came to help me; and I remained there with the kings of Persia.*
>
> *Daniel 10:12*

This passage clearly describes what happens to our prayers that have (seemingly) gone unanswered. Daniel had been praying and fasting for 21 days; finally on the 21st day the angel arrived with Daniel's deliverance and answer to his prayers. The angel informed Daniel that God had heard him and released the answer to his prayer the first time he prayed. Likewise, you must understand that when you pray according to the Word of God, the Lord also releases the answer to your prayers the very first day you pray. What holds up or hinders our prayers is the same thing that hindered Daniel's prayer.

> *For we wrestle not against flesh and blood, but against principalities, against powers, against the rulers of the darkness of this world, against spiritual wickedness in high places.*
>
> *Ephesians 6:12*

This passage shows us the different levels of principalities and demonic powers we fight against. When you pray, God releases the answers to your prayers. Once they are released, they must get through several levels of spiritual demonic resistance before they arrive to us.

Depending on Satan's strategy and attack against your life, your prayers are sometimes met with serious resistance by demonic principalities and powers in high places. The angel that was assigned to bring Daniel's answer was hindered by a principality that was assigned over that nation. There are demonic spirits assigned to every person, home, church, city, state, nation, and continent. The higher the level, the stronger the demonic opposition. Daniel's prayer was hindered by one of the highest demonic oppositions.

What was it that caused Daniel's angel to finally break through with the answer to his prayers? It was the fact that Daniel's angel received help from a hierarchy warrior angel. You have some angels that are messengers and some that are warriors. Messenger angels are assigned to deliver messages. Gabriel is a messenger angel.

Whenever you find Gabriel in the Bible, he is always de-
livering a message. Michael is a warrior angel. Whenever
you find Michael, he is always warring.

When the Air Force is planning to strike a position
where there is suspected air resistance, they send out
two waves of planes. They send out both bomber planes
and fighter jets. The bomber planes are assigned to carry
the bombs and drop them on their assigned positions.
The fighter jets are assigned to escort the bomber planes
and fight on their behalf in case of an attack. Even
though bomber planes have some weapons, they cannot
compare with the firepower and weaponry arsenal that
is on a fighter jet.

In the same example, the messenger angels can be
compared to the bomber planes, and the fighter jets can
be compared to the warrior angels. Just as the bomber
planes have some degree of weaponry, the messenger
angels are still strong and mighty. Many times they fight
and actually break through lines of demonic opposition
and resistance.

When you stand strong in your persistent prayer and
confession of the Word of God concerning your needs,
you empower even the messenger angels to break
through lines of resistance and bring you the answer to
your prayer. But sometimes your case may be like the
case of Daniel where there was strong demonic resistance and opposition. In Daniel's case, the messenger angel (who represents the bombers) had to call for Michael,
a warrior angel, who represents the fighter jets.

When you pray and confess the Word of God, God
releases the answers to your prayers to the messenger
angels. If it seems that your prayers have not been answered, the problem is not that God has not sent the an-

swer, the problem is that your prayers have been held up by demonic resistance. In this case, you need more than the key of prayer; you need the key of fasting and prayer. When you fast and pray, you are not only building up your spiritual muscles, but through prayer and fasting you are calling upon the warrior angels to come against any resistance to your answers.

> *In those days I Daniel was mourning three full weeks. I ate no pleasant bread, neither came flesh nor wine in my mouth, neither did I anoint myself at all, till three whole weeks were fulfilled.*
>
> *Daniel 10:2-3*

I think that we can safely assume that Daniel prayed before he began fasting and praying. We are to do the same thing. We pray and stand on God's Word; but when there is resistance, we initiate a fast along with our prayers. We do not know how long Daniel prayed for an answer before he began fasting, but what we do know is that he fasted and prayed for 21 days.

When you fast and pray, God not only sends out the messenger angels with the answer to your prayers, He also assigns the warrior angels to stand ready in case the messenger angels come up against strong resistance. Daniel's initial prayer released the messenger angels, but when he began prayer and fasting, it released the warrior angels to also stand ready.

It's the same way with us. When you fast along with your prayer, God assigns warrior angels that are able to (with your continued fasting and prayer) break through even the toughest lines of demonic hindrances and resistance, and bring your deliverance and answers to your prayers.

Chapter 4

When the Enemy Is Dug In

Deliverance From Strongholds

W e have already discovered in the previous chapter how fasting and prayer helps us when the enemy tries to hinder us from receiving the answer to our prayers. But what if the issue is a personal problem, temptation, or addiction? Many Christians believe that prayer alone should be enough to overcome any temptation, problem, or addiction of the enemy. This is true, unless the enemy has managed to get a stronghold in that area.

A military stronghold is an area where the opposing force has managed to get a stockpile of equipment, ammunition, firepower, and personnel in that particular position. It also represents an area where the enemy has had time to get fortified and well dug in. Once an enemy has managed to get dug in, it becomes much more difficult to get them out. In World War II, when our American forces tried to land on Normandy, Omaha Beach, the Air Force and Navy first bombarded the seashore for hours upon hours with relentless mortar and artillery fire. Yet after all that bombing, later, when our soldiers tried to come ashore, they were met with stiff resistance, and it took many hours of rigorous fighting, and the loss of thousands of lives to overtake Omaha Beach.

The reason why our bombardment seemed to be ineffective was because the enemy had months to dig underground shelters and reinforce them with steel and concrete. While our bombs were hitting some of their areas and doing some damage, they did not completely destroy their positions because the enemy was so well dug in.

It's the same way in the spiritual realm. If you are having trouble overcoming a temptation or addiction, it's not that your prayers are not effective; the problem is that the enemy has managed to get dug in. In these kinds of cases, it not only takes prayer, but it also takes fasting along with prayer to dig the enemy out.

And when they were come to the multitude, there came to him a certain man, kneeling down to him, and saying, Lord, have mercy on my son: for he is a lunatic, and sore vexed: for ofttimes he falleth into the fire, and oft into the water. And I brought him to thy disciples, and they could not cure him. Then Jesus answered and said, O faithless and perverse generation, how long shall I be with you? how long shall I suffer you? bring him hither to me. And Jesus rebuked the devil; and he departed out of him: and the child was cured from that very hour. Then came the disciples to Jesus apart, and said, Why could not we cast him out? And Jesus said unto

*them, Because of your unbelief: for verily I say
unto you, If ye have faith as a grain of mustard
seed, ye shall say unto this mountain, Remove
hence to yonder place; and it shall remove; and
nothing shall be impossible unto you. <u>Howbeit
this kind goeth not out but by prayer and fasting.</u>*

Matthew 17:14-21

In this passage, a man had brought his son to the disciples to cast a devil out of him. Although the disciples
had been walking in the miraculous and had experienced a degree of success in healing the sick and casting
out devils, they could not cast this one out. The man
eventually brought his son to Jesus who immediately
cast the devil out. In their astonishment, the disciples
asked Jesus why they could not cast this devil out. Jesus
gave them two reasons: First, a lack of their faith; and
secondly, because this kind (of stronghold) required a
life of fasting and prayer to be able to cast it out.

It was not that the devil was stronger than the Spirit
of God that was on the inside of them; it was because the
devil was dug in. Again, a stronghold is when the devil
has managed to dig in. This doesn't just apply to sinful
areas and areas of addiction; a stronghold can be in any
area. You can have a stronghold in an area of sin, sickness, poverty and lack, or just about in any area of your
life. Again, your inability to overcome Satan in a particular area has nothing to do with Satan's power—because
the power of God (within you) is greater than the power
of any demon, devil, or demonic power. The problem is
the fact that Satan has managed to get dug in.

Fasting and prayer breaks the stronghold grip of Satan and digs him out, allowing you to get the strength and victory to overcome him.

> *Is not this the fast that I have chosen? To loose the bands of wickedness, to undo the heavy burdens, and to let the oppressed go free, and that ye break every yoke?*
> *Isaiah 58:6*

This scripture describes exactly what we have been talking about regarding the enemy being dug in. When you fast, it lifts the enemy's cover, loosens his grip, digs him out, and breaks his hold. If Satan has beguiled you to believe or feel that you cannot overcome the struggles of temptations and addictions, he has lied to you. There is something you can do—fast!

Most of us have seen the game of tug-of-war played at picnics and recreational events throughout the years. Tug-of-war is not a game of strategy, but a conquest of strength. Whichever side is the strongest is the side that will win. We discovered in a previous chapter that we are made up of spirit, soul, and body. Whether you know it or not, there is a constant tug-of-war being waged within you. There is a constant fight between your flesh and your spirit. Your soul is in the middle of the struggle and will side with whichever one is the strongest.

Fasting is called afflicting the soul. When you fast, you bring affliction to your flesh and to your soul. Your soul consists of your mind, emotions, and your will (or resistance). When a person is bound by a temptation or addiction, it means that their mind, emotion, and will have been taken captive by the flesh. When the flesh becomes strong enough, it takes the soul captive. When the soul becomes captive to the flesh, it becomes weak and powerless to resist the lusts, wants, and desires of the flesh.

> *Submit yourselves therefore to God. Resist the devil, and he will flee from you.*
>
> *James 4:7*

Many people think that we resist the devil with our sheer will. Many look at this passage and only pay attention to the latter part of it that says, *"Resist the devil, and he will flee from you."* But if you want to be able to resist the devil, you must also pay attention to the first part of this passage where it says, *"Submit yourself to God."*

Most people that are bound by an addiction do not truly want to be bound in their hearts. But because their flesh is in control, they are helpless to the desires and wants of their flesh. In essence, they become slaves to the flesh. They have moments of strength where they try to fight back and resist their flesh, but because their flesh is so strong and dominant, their soul is weak and the battle of resistance becomes futile and often non-existent.

If a person is bound by a temptation or addiction, it means that the flesh side of the tug-of-war game within them is strong and mighty, and the spirit side of the tug-of-war game is weak. Again, whichever side is the strongest is the side to which the soul becomes subjected.

Prayer and confession of the Word of God are Keys to the Kingdom that can help strengthen the spirit-man. But if a person is praying for deliverance from a problem or addiction and still finds themselves helpless to the control and lusts of the flesh, it means that the balance of power within them still weighs heavily on the side of the flesh. But when you fast along with prayer, you dramatically change the balance of power. Fasting and prayer weakens the flesh, while at the same time strengthens your spirit-man.

Fasting shifts the balance of power and dominance from the flesh to the Spirit-man. When the balance of power in the tug of war within a person shifts from the dominance and control of the flesh to the strength and dominance of the spirit-man, the soul then comes under the influence of the spirit, and therefore becomes freed from the bondage of slavery and addictions of the flesh.

When this happens, we get the deliverance of Isaiah 58:6: We become *"loosed from the bands of wickedness; heavy burdens are lifted from us; we become freed from demonic oppression, and the yokes of slavery and addiction to the flesh become broken."*

If you or someone you know has been bound by the slavery of a temptation or addiction, don't allow the flesh to continue to win the tug-of-war game. Bring affliction to the flesh and discipline to the soul through fasting. And when you do so, you will bring strength to your spirit-man, and victory to your life.

Chapter 5

The Process and Length of Fasting

The Countenance of Fasting

Moreover when ye fast, be not, as the hypocrites, of a sad countenance: for they disfigure their faces, that they may appear unto men to fast. Verily I say unto you, they have their reward. But thou, when thou fastest, anoint thine head, and wash thy face; that thou appear not unto men to fast, but unto thy Father which is in secret: and thy Father, which seeth in secret, shall reward thee openly.

Matthew 6:16-18

The countenance of fasting refers to your look and demeanor while you are fasting. In the above passage Jesus referred to the Pharisees as hypocrites because they intentionally saddened their faces so that people would know they there were fasting and regard them as highly spiritual men of God.

While you are fasting, let your countenance be that of a child of God with the joy and peace of God upon you. Fasting is an affliction of the soul; but do not let the wearying of your soul affect your countenance. In other words, do not advertise the fact that you are fasting upon your face.

While some people are fasting, they look, as the saying goes, "like they have lost their best friend." While you are fasting, put a smile on your face and let the joy of the Lord shine through. Some people believe that this passage is saying that you cannot let anyone know you are fasting, but this is not what this passage is saying.

There will be times while you are fasting that people will offer you food, such as a relative, friend, or even a co-worker, and they will not understand why you are turning them down. Sometimes it will become necessary to simply let them know you are fasting, rather than to keep avoiding answering questions of why you do not want anything to eat. When people keep offering you food, there is no harm in letting them know that you are fasting, as long as your motive is not to intentionally let them know so as to look super spiritual before them.

How Often Should We Fast?

There are certain requirements or commandments that God has placed upon us such as loving one another, giving the tithe, and so forth. But there are also other things in which the Lord leaves up to us, such as giving of our free-will offerings and fasting. There is nowhere in the Bible where the Lord commands someone to fast. It's a free-will sacrifice unto the Lord. As to what type and duration of the fast, God leaves it up to us.

> *Obey them that have the rule over you, and sub-*
> *mit yourselves: for they watch for your souls...*
> *Hebrews 13:17*

While there are no directives that God gives us as to when, what type, or how long to fast, He does tell us to obey our spiritual leaders. If your pastor gives instructions for your church to fast, try to the best of your ability to abide by his directives concerning the fast. If you are unable to maintain and complete the fast according to his instructions, I suggest that you talk with your pastor or pastoral staff about permitting you to go on a lesser type of fast. As you read this book, you will learn about different types of fasts that may be more applicable and relative to your particular situation or ability.

Fasting is something that you grow into as you grow in the Lord. As you grow in the Lord, your hunger and desire will grow more for Him. You will also become more sensitive to His Spirit and His voice. As you do so, He will begin to lead you as to when, what type, and how long to fast.

Living A Fasted Life

"Routine Fasting"

> *But I keep under my body, and bring it into sub-*
> *jection...*
> *1 Corinthians 9:27*

If your pastor does not have a routine fast for your church, I strongly suggest that you learn to lead a fasted life. When I say fasted life, I'm talking about routine fasting. Routine fasting is to take a certain day each week and fast that day. For example, my church fasts each week from dinner Thursday to dinner Friday. This is probably the easiest type of 24 hour fast you can undertake. Because we can eat dinner Thursday, the only meals we actually miss are breakfast and lunch on Friday.

Living a fasted (routine fasted) life will help you in several areas. First, in case you go through a crisis or serious situation in your life and need to fast, your body and soul will already be accustomed or trained to fast. There are many people who experience different types of crises in their lives and attempt to go on a fast, but don't make it past the first meal because they are not accustomed to fasting.

When I was in the military we had to endure hardship weather, living, eating, and sanitation conditions when we went out to train and play war games. Believe it or not, there were some soldiers that felt that these conditions were cruel and unnecessary. However, I understood that training in these conditions was to help us to become somewhat acclimated to the hardship conditions of war, in case we had to actually go to war.

We have already discovered that fasting is a type of warring of the soul. Routine fasting is a way of continually training and disciplining your soul. And, like the military, if you do it routinely, you will be somewhat prepared when it becomes necessary to fast because of a storm or crisis in your life.

Each week you fast, take one or two particular issues

and fast about those things. For example: One week you may want to fast for your unsaved children or spouse. The next week you may want to fast for health issues in your life or one of your family member's lives, and so on. However, if you have a stronghold problem such as alcohol, drugs, gambling, sexual sins, pornography, overeating, or any other type of obvious stronghold or addiction, you should fast and pray about these types of issues each time you fast.

In addition to the weekly routine fast, I also recommend going on a two-day or three-day fast once a quarter (every three months). This can be an absolute fast, a normal fast, or whatever type of fast your faith is able to sustain. These and other types of fasts will be discussed more in depth in chapter nine.

Again, there are two purposes for going on routine fasts. One purpose is to keep you in spiritual shape. In the scripture beginning with this topic, Paul said, *"I keep under my body..."* In one of our previous topics, we found that the older should serve the younger. This means that our body and soul should be in subjection to, and led by our spirit. But this is not an automatic process.

It doesn't happen just because you want it to happen. Neither does it happen simply because you are born-again and attend church. You must work on it. If you want your spirit-man to rule and dominate your flesh, there is some work you must do.

It takes much prayer, reading of the Word of God, confessing the Word of God, leading a disciplined life, and fasting in order for you to keep your body under the subjection and control of your spirit-man. The reason why so many Christians are held in bondage and con-

trolled by the flesh is because they do not work on keeping their body under subjection. Routine fasting once a
week, and a two or three day fast once a quarter will
help you to keep your flesh under control. And instead
of being dictated by the craves and lusts of your flesh,
you will be led by your spirit instead.

Chapter 5

The Purpose of Fasting

1. To Get Directions From God and Clearly Hear His Voice

"As they ministered to the Lord, and fasted, the Holy Ghost said . . ."

Acts 13:2

How many times have we made the wrong choices and decisions in major areas that were detrimental and catastrophic to our lives? It's one thing to make a mistake in minor decisions that only affect our day, a few days, or a few dollars. But it's another thing to make the wrong choices and decisions about things that can change the course of, and even alter our entire lives.

Sometimes we make the mistake of making decisions based upon how things look to us in our natural senses. We often decide between jobs based upon which one pays the most. We go into marriages based upon how nice and kind the person seems to be, or even how the person looks. We make investments into businesses, as well as other types of investments based upon an open window of opportunity. We make major purchases such as cars, homes, and other major items based upon our emotions, greed, and a desire to impress others.

You should never make a major decision such as these without fasting about it first. When you make major decisions without fasting, you can allow the devil to come in and deceive you. We know that Satan is the thief that comes to steal, kill and destroy. One of the ways he steals, kills and destroys our lives is through deception.

When we do not fast when making major decisions, we can easily create what I call "Ishmaels." Ishmael was the first son of Abraham. God had promised Abraham a son. But as time went on and days and weeks turned into years and decades, Abraham found himself and his wife old and yet still had not received the promise of their son.

In their own carnal thinking, Abraham and his wife Sarah came up with an idea in which they could have a child and help fulfill God's promise. Sarah took her handmaiden and allowed Abraham to be intimate with her. She then became pregnant and gave birth to a son whose name was Ishmael.

Ishmael was not God's plan nor promise for their lives. Ishmael was a product of Abraham's carnal thinking and reasoning (a product of their flesh). Abraham and Sarah eventually found that they had missed God, and had still not received God's promise and plan for them concerning their son. They eventually learned how to trust God and wait on Him. Eventually after many errors and mistakes, they finally gave birth to their true son and promise from God by the name of Isaac.

When we do not seek the face of God for his directions, instructions, and guidance for our lives, we often make the same mistake that Abraham and Sarah did. We also create Ishmaels in our lives. There are many Christians with Ishmael marriages, Ishmael jobs, Ishmael homes and cars, and other imitations of the true blessings of God.

If we simply prayed and fasted, we would not become seduced into making fleshly decisions, because fasting helps us to hear the true voice and direction of the Lord.

Does Fasting Cause God to Speak to Us?

Fasting does not cause God to speak to us. If we truly pray according to His Word, He will speak to us. The question is not whether or not God will speak to us; the true question is this: When He does speak to us, will we be in a place and position where we can clearly hear and understand His true voice of directions and instructions for our lives, or will we be in a place where Satan can easily deceive us by disguising his voice as the voice of God?

> *And when He [the Lord] putteth forth His own sheep, He goeth before them, and the sheep follow Him: for they know His voice. And a stranger [Satan] will they not follow, but will flee from him: for they know not the voice of strangers.*
>
> *John 10:4-5*

The voice of the stranger is Satan using our natural minds to deceive us into going after Ishmael instead of

Isaac. Again, fasting does not cause God to speak to us. Fasting causes us to become sensitive to hear what God has been speaking all the time.

In 1 Kings 19:11-12, the Prophet Elijah wanted to hear a Word from God. First there came a tumultuous wind that tore apart the rocks. Elijah thought that God was in the wind, but He was not there. Next, there came an earthquake. For sure he thought God would be in the earthquake, and yet He was not there. Then came a fierce, fervent fire, but the voice of God was still not found in the fire. Finally, the voice of the Lord came to him in a still, small voice.

When you ask the Lord for directions, He will speak to you, but you must be in a place where you can hear His still, small voice. There are a lot of voices that constantly bombard us. You have to deal with the voice of your flesh, the voice of your wants and desires, the voice of carnal reasoning, the voice of Satan, and the voice of the Lord. The voice of the Lord is the softest and quietest of all the voices. And, unless you get in a place where you can hear the still, small voice of the Lord, you can easily be deceived into thinking you are hearing the voice of the Lord, when you are actually hearing one of the other voices instead.

It's like being in a noisy football stadium trying to hear someone on a cell phone. While everyone is talking and yelling, it would be very difficult to hear the person on the cell phone. If you wanted to hear that person, you would need to get in a quiet area to hear them and clearly distinguish the voice on the cell phone from the other voices around you.

When you fast and pray, it's like getting away from all the other voices and getting in a quiet place where the still, small voice of the Lord becomes clearer and easier to recognize and distinguish from the other voices.

2. To Help You Deny Yourself and Overcome Sin and Strongholds

When we become born-again, God places us into the family of God, sets us free from the strongholds and clutches of Satan, and gives us the power to overcome the enemy. If this is true, why then do so many Christians struggle with various strongholds and addictions?

The answer is because they have not been transformed. In Romans 12:2, the Bible says, *"And be not conformed to this world: but be ye transformed by the renewing of your mind..."* We said earlier that our soul is like a child. If we do not train and discipline our soul, it will become spoiled. And instead of obeying the voice of God and following the leadership of the Holy Spirit within us, it will become more susceptible to the voice of Satan and give in to the temptations and seductions of the enemy instead. Fasting helps to transform and train the soul to follow the spirit instead of the flesh.

> *Then said Jesus unto his disciples, If any man will come after me, let him deny himself, and take up his cross, and follow me.*
> *Matthew 16:24*

Denying yourself is to discipline the soul and bring the flesh under subjection to your spirit. Fasting is a very effective way of denying yourself. When you successfully fast, you are denying the flesh its strongest crave and desire—food. When you do so, you are saying "no" to your soul and your flesh, and causing them to come under the subjection of your spirit. You are training and disciplining your soul and making your flesh do without something it desperately wants. And, if you can deny your soul and flesh from having its greatest need and desire, you will then be able to also say "no" to sin when you are tempted.

Have you ever seen a scene in a grocery or department store where a small child wanted something, and because the parent would not get it for the child, the child put on a scene and totally embarrassed the parent, causing the parent to give in to what the child wanted? I've seen scenes like this many times. And yet every time I see one like it, the same thought comes to my mind— who is the child and who is the parent? Who is in charge here? Who is training whom? I know that the parent is in charge, but it seemed more like the child was in control.

When you see scenes like this, it's indicative of the fact that the parent has not been training, teaching, and disciplining the child. Part of training and disciplining a child is to teach them that there are things they cannot have, and even a time and a place for the things they can have. A child must understand that "no" means "no." A spoiled child doesn't understand what "no" means. Neither do they understand what "wait" means. When they want something, they want it "now." But if the parent would begin to discipline the child and teach them that there are things they cannot have, as well as a time and place for the things they can have, they will not embarrass the parent when the parent says "no."

While you are fasting, like a child, your flesh and soul constantly whines like a spoiled brat, crying to eat. No matter how short or long your fast may be, and no matter what type of fast you may be on, your flesh and soul will whine and crave food, now more than ever. If you can stand and say "no" to your soul to food, like a child, it will learn to become submissive to your spirit. Then, when it desires and craves sin, and your spirit says "no," your soul will come under subjection and receive what the spirit says.

Many (even Christians) have been bound to the slavery of their spoiled soul and flesh to sin, lust, and various temptations because they have not disciplined the soul and body by saying "no" through fasting. When you are fasting, you are telling your soul that there will be a time to eat, but it must wait until the time you allow for it to eat. Therefore, when your soul becomes disciplined and accustomed to hearing no, it will also become disciplined and accustomed to hearing and receive "no" to sin and temptations.

3. To Abort the Attacks of the Devil

As you grow in the Lord and in sensitivity to His voice, there will be times when the Holy Spirit will lead you on a fast. When the Holy Spirit leads us on a fast, it is because of an attack of the devil against our lives that we cannot see. It could be an attack against us to attempt to draw us away from God, an attack to seduce us deep into sin, or even an attack upon our lives or one of our family members.

And the Lord said, Simon, Simon, behold, Satan hath desired to have you, that he may sift you as wheat: But I have prayed for thee, that thy faith fail not...

                               Luke 22:31-32

In the above passage Jesus forewarns Peter of an attack upon his life. If Jesus had not interceded for Peter, he may not have become the mighty apostle that he became. There are times when the enemy will launch an all out attack against us. It could be an attack against our marriage, finances, health, children, spouse, relative, job, or any other area. These attacks originate in the spiritual realm before they become manifested in the physical realm. The Holy Spirit will many times warn us of these attacks of the enemy and lead us on a fast to abort them.

If you are led to fast by the Holy Spirit, you cannot wait until a convenient time and meal to fast. You cannot decide to wait until the next morning, or to go on one type of fast if the Holy Spirit is directing you on another. You must begin it at the time the Holy Spirit directs you, as well as the specific type of fast in which He leads you. Waiting until the next morning or for a more convenient time for you to fast could be too late.

I know of an intercessor that the Lord lead to go on a fast Thanksgiving day with the Thanksgiving dinner prepared and family on their way. While everyone else was eating turkey and dressing, she drank water and prayed. Little did she know that the devil was trying to kill her husband. The very next day he had a massive heart attack. His heart completely stopped beating and he stopped breathing, but he was miraculously revived and came back to life. Had she been disobedient and not fasted, he may not have lived pass that attack.

We live in the physical realm and cannot see the spiritual traps and the fiery arrows of attack that Satan aims against us. But God sees every one of them. And, if we would fast and pray when the Lord leads us, the Lord will preserve us and keep his weapons and attacks from prospering against us.

4. As A Sign of Godly Remorse for Your Sins

...the children of Israel were assembled with fasting... and stood and confessed their sins...
Nehemiah 9:1-2

One of the laws of physics is that for every action there is an opposite reaction. The same principal also applies to the spiritual realm. The Bible says the same thing, but in a different way. In Galatians 6:7, the Bible says, *"...for whatsoever a man soweth, that shall he also reap."* We blame the devil for many of our difficulties and trials of life, when in fact, many times we are simply reaping the thorns of sin and transgressions we have sown.

Many people walk in constant sin, disobedience, and rebellion against God and His Word. And like Jonah, they do not turn to God and repent of their sins and cry out to Him until He sends the storm of trouble their way. In fact, some of the storms we experience in life are not sent by the devil, but by God. It wasn't Satan that sent the storm and fish against Jonah; it was God. God sends the storm against us for a different purpose than that of Satan.

When Satan sends storms against us, they are always

to either destroy our lives or to destroy our hope, faith, and confidence in God just as Satan attempted to do with Job. But when God sends storms our way, they are always to get us to repent and turn to Him or draw us closer to Him. The storm that God sent against Jonah caused him to do just that. Not only did Jonah repent of his rebellion against God, he also became willing and obedient to do what God had originally told him to do.

If you have backslidden or walked in continual sin, disobedience, or abominations against the Lord, it's not a matter of "if" you will reap what you have sown, but "when." But if you would allow the conviction of the Holy Spirit to turn your heart to God and repent and fast, like Nineveh, you too can avoid experiencing the judgment hand of God against your life.

Fasting serves as a sign of the true sincerity of your repentance. When Jonah was sent to take the message to Nineveh, the purpose was to get them to repent of their sins. When Jonah finally obeyed the voice of God and gave the message to Nineveh, the people repented and fasted, and thereby avoided the calamity and destruction that was headed their way as a result of their sins.

Don't be like Jonah, who waited for the storm to come against him before he repented and changed. When the Holy Spirit brings conviction upon your heart because of your continued sin or gross sins, do like the people of Nineveh and not only repent, but fast and pray the prayer of repentance. You too can then be spared from the storm of God's judgment that may have been headed your way.

5. To Get Deliverance From an Attack of the Enemy

In a previous chapter, we talked about what happens in the spiritual realm when you fast. If you have been praying for deliverance from an attack of the enemy for a prolonged period of time, and have not received it, it means that the devil has managed to get a stronghold (dug in) in your life in that area.

It could either be as a result of negligence on your part, or simply an outright attack of the devil. It could be an attack on your health, finances, children, marriage or any other area of your life.

Remember, as we discussed earlier, when you pray, God sends the answer. If you have been praying for your healing or for some other type of deliverance, God has sent the answer. If you don't have your deliverance yet, it's because the answer has been held up in the spiritual realm. When you fast and pray, God sends the warrior angels that are able to break through demonic lines of resistance and bring your deliverance.

6. To Draw Close to the Lord

Therefore also now, saith the LORD, turn ye even to me with all your heart, and with fasting, and with weeping, and with mourning: And rend your heart, and not your garments, and turn unto the LORD your God...

Joel 2:12-13

We discovered in our previous point that fasting and

repentance can spare you from the judgment hand of God that may be against you because of your sins. But sometimes it may not have been that you were embedded in sin, your situation may be that you are just not as close to the Lord as you would like or need to be.

We have all at one time or another become a victim of allowing the devil the cause us to drift away from the Lord. It could be something as simple as you not spending quality time with God in prayer like you once did. It could be that you are allowing little things in your life that may not necessarily be sins, but yet at the same time things you know that are not pleasing to God. Your situation may even be such as when Jesus told the Church of Ephesus, *"You've lost your first love."* It could be that you are saying that you love God with your mouth, but you don't really sense the true love you once had in your heart for Him.

Each of these situations are forms of backsliding. Many people see a backslider as a person who has gone back to doing some of the ungodly or immoral things they once did before becoming a Christian such as drinking, taking drugs, committing fornication, adultery, or other things. But the truth is that a backslider is simply someone who has taken a step back from the Lord from a place that God had once taken them.

If you once prayed for an hour a day, and now you find yourself only praying once every two or three days for a few minutes, you are a backslider. If you once enjoyed coming to the house of the Lord to hear the Word of God, but now you don't enjoy going to church anymore and make excuses for not going, you are a backslider. If you once took time each day to study God's Word and hide His Word in your heart, and now you don't have time anymore for His Word, you are a back-slider.

If you are a backslider (regardless of what level of backsliding you may view yourself), you have become spiritually sick. When a person becomes sick, they loose their appetite. When you become spiritually sick, you loose your appetite for God and the things of God. Fasting brings affliction to the soul and flesh — while at the same time brings healing to the spirit. It will restore your joy in the Lord — which is your strength. It will create an appetite in your heart for the things of God, and bring you back to your first love and intimacy with the Lord.

Fasting For the Lives of Others

Fasting does not only work for your life; it also works for the lives of others for whom you pray and fast. Regardless of whether it's your spouse, children, parent, sibling, a Christian friend, or even a co-worker, begin to fast for them. It can be a stronghold of drugs, alcohol, sickness and disease, or any other kind of stronghold or addiction. You can help to set them free from Satan's grip in their lives by fasting for them.

Fasting does not only remove Satan's grip and stronghold against them regarding sin and addictions, it will also remove Satan's hindrance in their lives to keep them from receiving Christ. We all want to see our relatives and friends receive Christ and become born-again. Many of us pray for them on a daily basis. But if you really and truly want to see them receive Christ, don't just pray for them, break Satan's stronghold grip of hindrance upon their lives by fasting for them.

Chapter 7

Things to Abstain From While Fasting

Many Christians fast, but do not accomplish their spiritual goal from their fast. One of the reasons why they do not accomplish their goal is because they allow the devil to get them out of focus while they are fasting. In order to keep your focus and not allow the devil to distract you, there are some things you should avoid or abstain from while fasting. These are just a few of them. As you grow more in the Lord and in sensitivity to His voice, the Holy Spirit will give you more direction.

1. Television and Movies

All things are lawful unto me, but all things are not expedient: all things are lawful for me, but I will not be brought under the power of any.
1 Corinthians 6:12

We all know that it's not a sin to watch (clean) television programs and movies. But while you are fasting, even though it may not be a sin, it will distract you, take you away from your focus, and nullify the spiritual effects and accomplishments of fasting.

Television and movies, as well as other secular entertainment only serve to entertain, profit, and strengthen the flesh and the soul. And, since the goal of fasting is to strengthen the spirit-man, watching television and movies will get you in the flesh instead of in the spirit, and can cause your fast to become counterproductive.

You can however watch Christian television programs such as TBN and other inspirational networks and shows. But you must be careful not to give in to the temptation to channel surf while you are tuning in to your Christian channels.

I'm sure that you are very familiar with the location of Christian television stations on your cable or satellite system. If you begin channel surfing, the devil will make sure that you come across something that you really would love to see. It might be one of your favorite shows, a highly anticipated sports event, or a movie you've been waiting for weeks or even months to see. And if you give in to the temptation to watch it for a moment, you will find yourself glued there, and the moments will turn into minutes and hours.

2. Music

Speaking to yourselves in psalms and hymns and spiritual songs, singing and making melody in your heart to the Lord; Giving thanks always for all things unto God and the Father in the name of our Lord Jesus Christ;

Ephesians 5:19-20

While you are fasting, do not listen to any music (including gospel music) that does not (clearly) worship, glorify, and exalt Lord. You should abstain from all jazz, classical, and any other non-Christian music during your fast. I suggest praise and worship music, or music and songs that you know will draw your heart to God, and encourage you to think upon and bless the Lord.

You need to also abstain from all upbeat gospel music. I have nothing against different types of upbeat gospel music, as well as untraditional gospel music such as gospel rap, gospel rock, and acid gospel. These types of gospel music can be very encouraging and inspiring to those who love it. However, during your fast, you should abstain from these types of music.

Even though there is spiritual edification and encouragement that can come from listening to these types of gospel music, they can sometimes entertain our flesh more than uplift our spirit. When you are fasting, you need to abstain from these types of music because you want to keep away from anything that will entertain your soul or flesh. During your fast you want to focus on music that will (clearly) uplift, build, and strengthen your spirit-man. As you seek the Lord and pray about what type of music to listen to, the Lord will lead and guide you.

3. Sexual Intimacy

Defraud ye not one the other, except it be with consent for a time, that ye may give yourselves to fasting and prayer...

1 Corinthians 7:5

Many people would think, "What in the world could fasting possibly have anything to do with having sexual intimacy with your spouse?" It's not that sex is wrong; on the contrary. If you are married, the bedroom is holy and undefiled unto the Lord. But sex is a totally fleshly, carnal, soulish act. Sex brings pleasure to the flesh and the soul, but does nothing whatsoever for the spirit. And, the purpose of the fast is to war against the flesh and discipline the soul, while exercising and building up the spirit-man. Therefore, all sexual intimacy should be avoided during fasting.

You should also let your spouse know that you are preparing to fast so that they won't inadvertently tempt you. If you and (or) your spouse are not able to refrain from sexual intimacy for a long time, it would be best if you kept your fast to a minimum number of days.

4. Taking Care of Business

During a long fast, you can go ahead and take care of your business as you normally would do. However, during a short fast of two days or less, try to abstain from spending too much time taking care of non-essential business. If you must take care of essential business, do not feel convicted about doing it; it's all right. But if you know that you are going on a short fast, try to take care of your business prior to starting your fast.

The purpose behind this is that your soul is looking for anything that can take its time or attention away from the Lord while you are fasting. Again, the soul gets nothing out of fasting. So while you are fasting, your soul will want you to spend the entire time paying bills, cleaning the house, taking care of needed chores, or anything else to distract you from the purpose of your fast, which is to spend quality time with the Lord and draw closer to Him.

When you begin fasting, your mind will think of a thousand things you could be doing. Don't give into the temptation of just being busy simply to pass time while you are fasting. Purpose in your heart that you are not only going to complete your fast, but you are also going to get something out of your fast by keeping your focus on the Lord.

5. Any Distractions

After reading the things in this chapter, you are probably saying to yourself, "I can't do anything while I'm fasting but pray spend time with the Lord." Well, that's kind of the purpose of fasting. Again, while you are fasting, you are denying your flesh and disciplining your soul. You are to deny yourself anything that is entertaining or pleasurable, while at the same time fill your time with things that will strengthen and build up your spirit-man.

If you just simply get bored stiff with spiritual things, and you need some form of entertainment, go to the video store and rent a Christian Movie. Video stores such as Blockbuster carry a wide array of Christian movies. This would also be a good time to get a good inspiring Christian book to read. I myself like short books of about 120 pages or less. If I want to read a book that has 120 pages or more, I wait until I am either traveling, or when I have some time to dedicate to it. During a fast is one of those times.

Reading a good Christian book will serve two purposes. It will provide some type of entertainment to the flesh – which is all right just as long as it is uplifting to your spirit. And, it will help you to increase your knowledge in something spiritual.

* NOTE: This chapter does not apply to the partial fast and the material fast. It is for the absolute, normal, or juice fast.

Chapter 8

Initiating the Fast

How to Begin Your Fast

When you fast, you are waging war against your flesh. That's why you can say that fasting is a form of warfare. A war never just happens. One side declares war on the other side. There is always a beginning and an end. Likewise, there should be an official beginning to your fast. Before you begin your fast, there are several things you should do.

1. Ask the Lord to Search Your Heart and Repent of Sin

Fasting and prayer can only be effective when your heart is pure and right with God. So before you begin your fast, make sure your heart is right. If it's not, you will not achieve the spiritual goal you are looking for in your fast. The way you get your heart right with God is by asking Him to search you. In Ps 139:23, David said, *"Search me, O God, and know my heart: try me, and know my thoughts."* David was asking God to search his heart and expose the sin and wickedness within.

Before you begin your fast, you should do the same thing. Ask the Lord to search your heart and reveal to you if there is unrepented sin in your life. And, whenever you truly and honestly ask the Holy Spirit to search your heart, He will reveal to you if there is any sin and wickedness within you.

In Psalms 19:12, David also asked the Lord to cleanse him from *"secret faults."* Secret faults are sins, iniquities, transgressions, and rebellion in your life that no one knows about but you and God. They are also things that may not necessarily be sin, but yet things in which you know displease God, but yet you still want to hold on to. When you truly ask the Lord to search your heart, the Holy Ghost will show you all these things. Once He shows them to you, it's up to you to come clean by repenting of them.

God is not looking for us to be perfect; He is only looking for us to be honest. And until you are willing to become honest and open with the Lord, you can pray and fast all you want, but you will never get what you are looking for from the Lord.

In James 4:2, the Bible says, *"We have not because we ask not, and because we ask "amiss."* To ask "amiss" is to ask the wrong or improper way. One of the ways we improperly ask of the Lord is to pray and ask Him for something without searching our hearts and repenting of our (obvious, as well as secret) sins. Don't let your fasting go in vain; ask the Lord to search and cleanse your heart by repenting of the things He shows you.

2. Set the Goals You Would Like to Achieve

Before you begin your fast, set your goals that you would like to obtain from your fast. Your first goal should always be to draw closer to the Lord and grow stronger in Him. If you properly fast, this is something that will automatically happen, but you must still make it a goal and verbalize it in your opening prayer and commitment to the Lord.

In addition to your spiritual goal, you should also have a physical goal. It can be deliverance from sickness or disease, deliverance for your children so that they can receive Christ, or deliverance from whatever the enemy is attempting to hinder in your life. If you are bound by a stronghold or addiction, you should always pray for deliverance from it during your fast.

3. Make Sure You Have the Resources You Need

I mentioned in one of our previous chapters that while fasting, it is all right to read books, watch Christian movies and programs, and other things that will inspire you in the Lord. Make sure you have these materials before you begin. You may also need to get some kind of reference book of scriptures to help you to make your confessions while you are on your fast. Our book, "The Weapons of Our Warfare, Volume III" is a book of scripture confessions that would be a good resource for you during your fast.

4. Pray and Sanctify Your Fast

Your fast does not begin when you finish eating your last meal before fasting; it begins when you sanctify it unto the Lord. You sanctify it by committing it unto the Lord and setting aside a specific time to begin your fast. If you do not set a specific time to begin your fast, the devil will try to get you to keep delaying your fast by telling you that you haven't officially began fasting yet.

When you commit it unto the Lord, you commit your start time and date, as well as your finish date and time unto Him. Ask the Lord to help you to endure and be committed to finish your fast. Let the Lord know the things you are fasting to achieve, and thank Him in advance for giving you deliverance and victory in those areas.

Different Ways of Being Led Into A Fast

You have two basic ways of being led into a fast. The first is the Spirit-led fast. The second is the Free-will fast.

1. Spirit Led Fasts

Then was Jesus led up of the Spirit into the wilderness to be tempted of the devil. And when he had fasted forty days and forty nights, he was afterward an hungered.

Matthew 4:1-2

This passage is taken from the familiar account of Jesus' temptation in the wilderness. The passage says that He was led by the Spirit. God knew of this encounter He was about to have with Satan, so He led Jesus on this fast to prepare Him.

The Spirit-led fast is just what the name describes; it's when the Holy Spirit leads you to fast. The Lord will lead you on Spirit-led fasts when you come to a point in your spiritual life where you learn how to clearly and distinctly hear the voice of God. They are normally inspired by the Holy Spirit to either prepare a person for a mighty work of the Lord, or prepare them for an all out attack of the enemy.

When I say an "all out attack," I am not only talking about temptations, but also other types of attacks. It can be an attack against your body, such as in the case of Satan attacking Job with sickness and disease. It can also be an attack against your life, or even an attack against the life of one of your family members or friends.

It is important that you learn how to be led by the Spirit so that the Lord can lead you on Spirit-led fasts. It's important because we cannot see in the spiritual realm, and neither can we see in the future. We cannot see the tricks, traps, and plans of attack that Satan has set against us. But even though we cannot see these attacks, God sees them. And, if we would fast when He leads us, we can come through Satan's attacks in victory and triumph.

2. Free Will Fasts

Free-Will fasts are by far the most common used by Christians. A free-will fast is one in which a person initiates a fast themselves without the Spirit of God leading them. They can be used for the same reasons as used in Spirit-led fasts, only, the person is the one who senses the need for the fast, and imposes the fast on themselves rather than the Holy Spirit leading them on it.

3. Corporate Fasts

And Jehoshaphat feared, and set himself to seek the LORD, and proclaimed a fast throughout all Judah.

2 Chronicles 20:3

This is a fast that is initiated by a leader such as a pastor, bishop, or any leader over a church or auxiliary. In a corporate fast the leader usually gives the directives as to the type of fast, the duration of the fast, and the things to pray for while on the fast. With corporate fasts, everyone is directed to fast and pray in unity, usually on the behalf of the church, organization, or auxiliary. There are other times that a pastor or leader will institute a corporate fast on the behalf of their city, state, nation, or even the body of Christ as a whole.

If you are a member of a church, and the pastor or leader calls a fast, because God commands us to obey those who have rule and authority over us, we are under obligation to comply with the directives of the fast. If you are unable to comply with your leadership in maintaining your fast, talk with your pastor, pastoral staff, or auxiliary leader about allowing you to go on a lesser type of fast.

Working and Fasting

Many people are taught that you cannot pray and fast while you are working. They teach that you must be locked up in a room somewhere with no contact with the outside world. Although that type of fasting is very effective, and in some cases of extreme crisis even necessary, with our jobs and other responsibilities in life, it may not always be possible to fast this way. Therefore, it is likely that most Christians will have to fast while they are working.

> *Pray without ceasing.*
> *1 Thessalonians 5:17*

The above passage tells us to pray without ceasing. This well-known passage is not talking about non-stop prayer; it is talking about the continuing attitude of prayer. The way you pray without ceasing is to pray before you start your work, on your lunch break, whenever you get your breaks, and as often as you can. It is to also periodically pray and rehearse the Word of God within your heart while you are working, as well as throughout your day.

While you are working, try to keep your mind upon the Lord, and upon the things of God as much as possible without jeopardizing your job. When I say, "without jeopardizing your job," I am referring to the point of losing your concentration on your work and making mistakes and errors. If this is your case, then reserve your moments of meditation to your lunch time and breaks.

While you are fasting, and at work, make a conscious effort to stay away from all gossip, backbiting, complaining, talking about co-workers, talking about the supervisors, management, or any type of negative conversations. Don't get involved in these types of conversations, and try your best to avoid being around people who constantly harp on these types of things. These types of conversations will cause your fast to become counterproductive.

If you have some type of job that allows you to listen to music (with or without headphones), take advantage of this opportunity. Take a walkman or radio to work with you and listen to Godly inspiring music (or messages) while you are working. If your job does not allow them, simply make music and melody in your heart unto the Lord periodically throughout your workday.

If your job consumes you to the degree that you find it impossible to focus upon the Lord at all, and you cannot take a break, take time for lunch, or take any time at all to get away, you may want to limit your fast to the weekend or your days off. Once again, the purpose of fasting is to focus on the Lord. If you have to work on a mind-consuming job with no lunch time or breaks, then you may need to reserve your fasting to weekends or your days off.

Chapter 9

Different Types of Fasts

Some people hear the word "fasting" and their minds automatically think about starving themselves on a long, hard 30-day fast without any food or water. However, there are different types of fasts. In this chapter we will discuss them. Regardless of the condition of your health, age, or work environment, you can at least go on one of these fasts.

The devil has deceived many people into thinking they cannot fast because of these, as well as other types of circumstances. But God has designed fasting in a way so that anyone can do it. You may not be able to go on some of the fasts listed in this section, but there is one for you.

Taking Something For Your Breath

While you are fasting, you must be especially careful to monitor your breath. Because you are not eating, your stomach acids will become more active, and your saliva will not go through its usual recycling process, causing your breath to become offensive.

Regardless of the type of fast, it is recommended that you take some kind of breath mint while you are out in public. But I caution you to be careful with mints. Because you are not eating anything else, your body will take to breath mints like they are a full course meal. You can find yourself overindulging in the candy to pacify your appetite more than taking it for your breath.

This is why I recommend having some type of small breath mint such as a tic-tac, rather than mint candy. It will soothe your breath, while at the same time not give you the satisfaction of eating candy.

1. The Supernatural Fast

* Caution: There have only been a handful of people throughout the history of mankind who have been able to successfully complete a supernatural fast. This fast is listed for information only, and is not a suggested method of fasting. It should not be undertaken or even attempted unless the Lord has "divinely" spoken to you to do so.

> *And he [Moses] was there with the LORD forty days and forty nights; he did neither eat bread, nor drink water...*
>
> *Exodus 34:28*

The Supernatural fast is one in which a person goes without any food, water, or any other kind of additional vitamins, nutrients or supplements for an exceptional amount of time (usually thirty to forty days).

In this passage, the Bible says that Moses was in the presence of the Lord for 40 days and 40 nights. God is the sustainer of life Himself. If a person comes in the true, divine presence of the Lord, He can sustain their body. This is what enabled Moses to live with no food or water for such a prolonged number of days.

Had it not been for God's presence and preservation upon Moses' body, he would have died after a few days. But because of God's presence upon him, his body was sustained in good health for forty complete days. This type of fast is ill advised for anyone without being led by the true presence and voice of God. There have been very few people in the history of mankind that have been able to successfully sustain this type of fast.

I once knew a pastor that sustained brain damage because they attempted to go on this type of fast of their own will and desire. While the pastor's intention and motive was good, it was still a lack of wisdom on their part to attempt this type of fast without the divine presence of God to sustain them. So once again, this type of fast is ill advised.

2. The Absolute Fast

And he [Paul] was three days without sight, and neither did eat nor drink.

Acts 9:9

The Absolute fast is similar to the Supernatural fast in that the person does not eat any food nor drink any water. The difference is that while the Supernatural fast can last up to forty days or more, the Absolute fast does not (normally) last longer than 3 days.

The body can go a number of days without food, but it cannot go long without water. The Bible therefore does not record any absolute fasts that go beyond 3 days, with the exception of several accounts of the Supernatural fast in which the person's body was sustained by the presence of God.

The caution that I would like to make about the absolute fast is that this fast should not be undertaken for more than three days. And, even then, only if you have a clear directive from the Lord, and you are in excellent health. If you have any type of questionable medical condition, consult your physician or consider another type of fast.

If you are taking medication that must be taken with food, eat a slice of bread or a few crackers. The Lord understands your condition and will still honor your fast. However, don't allow the temptation of needing to eat something with your medicine entice you to turn it into a meal.

3. The Normal Fast

". . . This is the fourteenth day that ye have tarried and continued fasting, having taken [not eaten] nothing."

Acts 27:33

This fast is called the normal fast because it is the most common method of fasting. Since we know the body cannot (under normal circumstances) go for 14 days without food and water, it is safe to assume that they drank water while on this fast. During this fast you do not eat foods of any kind, but you are allowed to drink water. This fast is good for many because it (unlike the absolute fast) allows you to go beyond three days because water will sustain your body longer.

Although this fast allows you to drink water, it must still be undertaken with caution. As with the Absolute fast, if you are fasting for longer than three days, make sure that you have a clear directive from the Lord and that you are in good health.

I also still give the same caution as with the Absolute fast: If you are taking medication that must be taken with food, eat a slice of bread or a few crackers. The Lord understands your condition and will still honor your fast. However, don't allow the temptation of needing to eat something with your medicine cause you to turn it into a meal.

4. The Juice and Liquid Fast

Acts 27:33

In this fast you do not eat any foods, but you are allowed to not only drink water, but also juices and other forms of liquid nutrients such as Ensure or blended fruits and vegetables. This is the recommended fast for people who would like to fast for longer than three days. It is still very effective because your stomach is still in a semi-state of fasting since it is not working to digest any solid foods. It is recommended because you can drink juices and other liquid nutrients that will help to keep your body healthy. It is a recommended fast for people who work on jobs that require strenuous work, or work outdoors in the heat.

There are people who have had operations on their stomach or intestines and have been put on this type of fast by their doctor for weeks. It is safe because the juices and liquid nutrients they drink help to supplement the vitamins and nutrients they would normally have received from eating food, allowing them to fast for a much longer period of time.

The body is made up of 80% liquid. Your body can go days without food, but can only go a short time without water or liquids. The Juice or Liquid fast allows you to go longer periods of time of fasting and still be able to work while you are fasting.

Since the purpose of this fast is to allow you to be able to have liquid nourishment, all non-essential liquids that do not provide vitamins and nourishment are prohibited. All liquids such as coffee, tea, hot chocolate, sodas, and other non-nutritional liquids should be avoided while you are on this fast.

The caution in this type of fast is to stay away from juices that have a high concentration of acids, such as orange, pineapple and grapefruit juices.

5. The Partial Fast

I ate no pleasant bread, neither came flesh nor wine in my mouth, neither did I anoint myself at all, till three whole weeks were fulfilled.
                                        Daniel 10:3

In this fast you are allowed to not only drink water and juices, but also eat certain kinds of foods. The purpose of this fast is to allow you to eat foods that will strengthen your body, allowing you to fast for prolonged periods of time. This fast allows you to still work on even the most stressful, strenuous, or heat climate jobs — allowing you to still be able to perform your work for an extended number of days.

If you notice, Daniel said, *"I ate no pleasant bread..."* Since the purpose for eating is nutrition, you are still to abstain from all pleasurable foods, snacks and liquids. This fast usually consists of vegetables, salads (without meat), bread, and juices. As with the liquid and juice fast, you can still drink juices and liquid nutrients, however, you should abstain from all types of meats, as well as coffee, sodas, candy, snacks or sweets of any kind. Basically, if it is either considered a snack or dessert, or something that appeases your appetite, you should not eat or drink it on this fast.

6. The Material Fast

This fast is different from all the other fasts mentioned thus far because during this fast you can eat or drink whatever you want. In this fast you do not fast from food or liquids, but from spiritual distractions.

Several years ago the Lord spoke to my heart about going on this type of fast. The Lord's instructions to me were to abstain from all carnal entertainment. This included all (non-Christian) television and music, as well as other forms of entertainment.

I had never heard of this type of fast before several

years ago when the Lord spoke to my heart about doing it. At that time I was an avid college football fan. I couldn't wait until Saturday afternoon college football. One Saturday while I was rushing home to watch television, the Spirit of the Lord spoke to me about going on a material fast for thirty days. Once I found that it was truly the Lord speaking to me, I remember saying to myself, "this is going to be easy." But I also remember after thinking about how easy this fast was going to be, that it also included my Saturday afternoon college football.

Even still, I remember thinking, "at least this will be much easier than going on one of the other types of fasts." The first day or two was easy, but by the end of the first week, it was a struggle. I found that I had made a habit out of coming home after work and cutting on the television. Many Christians would be surprised to know the stronghold that television has on their lives. And, going for a prolonged period without watching television is almost as difficult as some of the other above-mentioned fasts for some people.

During the time that I would have normally been watching television, I spent praying, reading and studying the Word of God. By the time the fast had ended, I found myself as strengthened as I had been when I had gone on some of the other types of fasts.

I found that the principle of fasting was not to simply go on a diet. It was to also discipline the soul and put the flesh under subjection. And whenever you do this, you strengthen the spirit-man. This fast not only brought strength to my spirit-man, it also broke my habit and compulsion of television.

The material fast may not be as effective for everyone as it was for me, and it may not be the most effective fast for every situation, but it did provide a degree of strengthening for me, and helped me to break my compulsion with television.

The material fast doesn't have to be television; it can be anything that becomes a compulsion, or something that consumes your time. To be effective, it has to be something that will be a real struggle for you to do without. To me it was television. To some it may be movies; to others it may be music. But whatever it is, if you can learn to say "no" to it for a few weeks and spend that time with the Lord, you will find yourself stronger, and you will be able to also say "no" to your flesh when it wants to have its way.

Chapter 10

Maintaining Your Fast

No Pain, No Gain

Although God does not give us specific directives as to the length of time and what type of fast we should undertake, I have a simple principle that I think will help you to set some standards. We have already discovered that fasting is like spiritual weight lifting. In weight lifting, there is a slogan that helps weight lifters to understand how much weight they should lift. The slogan is, "No Pain, No Gain."

When you lift weights, you can lift for either one of two reasons: The first is for toning muscles, and the second is for building muscles. If you only want to tone your muscles or burn fat, you lift an amount of weight that is somewhat comfortable to you to lift with a comfortable number of repetitions. For example: Most men who do not lift weights can go into a gym and lift several repetitions of 50 pounds of weight without much strain or serious effort.

If a man continually lifted several repetitions of 50 pounds he would begin to tone up his arms and chest muscles. This would result in him also losing weight (provided he was on some kind of diet program). But if he wanted to build muscle, he would have to lift more weight.

In order to build muscle, you must find a weight amount that is not too much for you to lift, and yet enough weight to cause you to put forth a serious amount of effort and energy. Once you began lifting this amount, your muscles will start building (over a period of time). Eventually your body will get used to lifting that amount of weight and will no longer build muscle. You would then need to increase the amount of weight you were lifting if you wanted to continue to build muscle.

So when they use the slogan, "No Pain, No Gain," what they are saying is that if it doesn't cause any "pain" — meaning a serious amount of effort, energy and exertion to lift, you will not "gain" any muscle.

In our previous chapter, we discovered that there are several types of fasts. After learning about the different types of fasts, it would be tempting to always pick the partial fast and material fast and stay with them. These types of fasts may be effective when you first begin fasting, or while fasting for long periods of time, but other than that, they may not be as effective as other types of fasts.

I believe that the same principle that works with weight lifting also works with fasting. If it doesn't cause you any pain you to fast, it may not give you much spiritual gain. For a person who is starting to fast for the first time, I suggest starting off fasting until twelve o'clock noon. After a little while, you can extend the fast to 3:00 p.m. Later, you can extend it until 6:00 p.m. As you continue to fast, you will be able to go on longer and more difficult fasts as the Lord leads. Soon you will find yourself able to fast for 24 hours, and later 2 or 3 days, or even longer.

Some people do not usually eat breakfast; so fasting until 12:00 noon would not give them much of a challenge. If you can go on a fast with little or no effort, then it may not give you the spiritual gain you are looking for. While it is not recommended that you over commit yourself to go on a fast that you do not have the faith to complete, at the same time you must go on fasts that will at least challenge your flesh. Again, "No Pain, No Gain."

The Consciousness of Food

When you fast, you have two enemies working against you—Satan and your flesh. While you are fasting, your senses will become more alert and heightened to all kinds of foods around you—even foods you don't normally like or eat. You may not even like a particular food or snack, but when you are fasting, even those kinds of foods and snacks will become as appealing to you as your favorite foods.

You will also become more conscious of mealtimes than ever before. I do not regularly eat breakfast. It's a meal I only eat once or twice a week. But when I am fasting, I wake up hungry and ready to eat breakfast. When you are not fasting, you can easily miss meals and not even be conscious of the fact that you have missed the meal. But, when you are fasting, it's like an alarm goes off in you to bring you notice of each and every meal you miss.

Satan will attempt to use this heightened sense of alertness and awareness of food to talk you into ending your fast early. So in essence, you have two enemies working against you and attempting to talk you out of continuing your fast—Satan and your flesh. But don't let them do all the talking; begin taking part in this conversation. Begin encouraging yourself. Tell yourself that you can make it. Start quoting scriptures such as *Philippians 4:13*, which says, ***"I can do all things through Christ who strengthens me."*** Once you begin to take part in this conversation, you will encourage yourself to continue on your fast.

People Working Against You

In the above topic we discovered that you have two enemies fighting against you when you fast. You have Satan talking to you and tempting you to break your fast, and you also have your flesh talking and fighting against you to break your fast. But that's not all of your opponents of fasting. In addition to those two enemies, you also have people who will (indirectly) fight against you and try to get you to break your fast early.

People can be used by the devil to help him hinder a Christian's life and not even know they are being used by him. To the person, they receive what they think is an innocent thought to do something and act upon that thought, not knowing that it came from Satan to hinder someone's life spiritually.

From that time forth began Jesus to show unto his disciples, how that he must go unto Jerusalem, and suffer many things of the elders and chief priests and scribes, and be killed, and be raised again the third day. Then Peter took him, and began to rebuke him, saying, be it far from thee, Lord: this shall not be unto thee. But he turned, and said unto Peter, Get thee behind me, Satan: thou art an offence unto me: for thou savourest not the things that be of God, but those that be of men.

Matthew 16:21-23

In this passage, Jesus had just finished telling the disciples that He was going to go to suffer the punishment of the cross. Satan then put in Peter's mind and heart to be concerned about Jesus' physical well-being and having to suffer and die. What he told Jesus, he told Him out of love, concern, and compassion for Him. But the source of the thought was demonic; it came from Satan. When Jesus said, "get thee behind me," He was not talking to Peter, but to the demonic spirit that gave Peter the thought. It was demonic because Satan was attempting to use Peter to discourage Jesus from fulfilling the divine plan of God — going to the cross. To Peter, he conceived a thought that seemed to be caring and considerate of Jesus, but it was still inspired by Satan to hinder Jesus from going to the cross.

Just as Satan tried to use Peter to hinder Jesus through what he thought was a thoughtful, considerate, innocent thought, Satan will attempt to use family members, friends, and co-workers in the same manner against you. There have been times that I have been fasting, and a person who has never offered to do anything for me in their life, decided to buy me lunch and bring it to me. There have been occasions where my supervisor called a meeting, but this time decided to have coffee and hot, fresh, tasty doughnuts for the meeting.

I remember several occasions of planning to go to my mother's house, and it just so happened that my mother called while I was out taking care of business. My wife told her that I was planning to go by her house when I finished. By the time I arrived at mom's house, she had prepared one of my favorite meals just for me. I have even had occasions where I had told my wife I was fasting, but she forgot I was fasting and fixed one of my favorite dishes.

In each of these accounts, my spouse, family members, friends and co-workers all thought they were doing something that was thoughtful and considerate, not knowing that they had received the thought from Satan to hinder my fast. As you fast, you too will experience occasions like some of these I have experienced. But understand that it's not the people, but the enemy behind the scenes influencing them to do it.

Getting Over the Hump

When I was in the military, we had physical training 3 to 5 times a week, which among other things involved a 3-5 mile run. At the time it seemed that there was nothing worse than getting out of my bed at 5 o'clock in the morning and running 3-5 miles.

Many people think that the most difficult part of running that long of a distance is the last couple of miles.

Although the last couple of miles were hard, the most difficult part of the run for me was the first mile. It seemed that after I had passed the first mile, the run became much easier.

I later learned what was happening physically. When you exercise, at first you are working off of sheer will and strength. But somewhere between 10 and 20 minutes of exercising, your body begins releasing a chemical called adrenalin. Adrenalin is a chemical that aids your body in exercising and strenuous work. It causes your heart to beat faster, and as your temperature rises, it also causes you to sweat—thereby helping to cool your body. After your adrenalin begins to flow, exercising becomes easier.

I've noticed that there is also a type of spiritual adrenalin that you also get when you fast. When you begin fasting for 3 days or longer, you will find that the most difficult part of your fast is the first day. Because of the difficulty most people experience with fasting for 24 hours, they cannot imagine themselves fasting for a longer period of time.

Your first day of fasting will seem like running up a steep hill. But by the second day your fast will get a lot easier, and it will seem like you are running on level ground. And, by the third day, it will seem like you are running down hill.

To some people, imagining themselves going on a three-day fast (or longer) would be like imagining themselves climbing Mt. Everest. But don't let Satan intimidate you and stop you from receiving what you need. The hardest part of completing a 3 day fast (or longer), is getting over the hump of the first day. If you can just get over the hump of the first day, you will find that your fast actually gets easier and not harder. By the middle of the second day your spiritual adrenalin will kick in, and you will be on your way to victory.

I'm not saying that there will not be any more struggle or temptation after the first day. In fact, I can assure you that there will be—because Satan does not want you to achieve your goal, and will fight you all the way to the end of your fast. But, what I am saying is that if you can make it past the first day (hump day), that you would have made it past the most difficult time of your fast and the hill will level off.

Chapter 11

If You Break Your Fast Early

Have You Made Any Progress If You Break Your Fast Early?

Many people teach that you have not spiritually gained anything if you break a fast early. I completely differ from this philosophy. As long as you have been doing what you should do on your fast (focusing on spiritual things and refraining from fleshly things), you have made spiritual progress regardless of how early you may have broken your fast.

It's like a person purposing in their heart to go on a diet and exercise program for six months and only accomplishing three months of it. Because they didn't complete their projected goal, does that mean that they did not make any progress with their body and health? Of course it doesn't. If they correctly dieted and exercised, they would have lost some weight, toned up some, and began to even make some improvement in their health.

Notice we said, "correctly dieted and exercised." If this person had been half-hearted in their diet and exercise program, then they probably would not have seen any results. But if they were serious and committed, they would have seen some progress.

It's the same way in the spiritual realm. If you have been focused on the spiritual things and properly fasted, then ending your fast early does not nullify the progress that you made while fasting. If you were attempting to go on a three day Normal Fast and only completed a day and a half of it, then your spirit-man profited a day and a half of that fast.

There is however a negative consequence that comes out of breaking a fast early. When you break a fast early, you will feel defeated in your mind. And, it's the strength of the mind, which is the soul that gives you the will to resist the devil. But know that you have defeated him for whatever time you did accomplish your fast. And, know also that you have made some accomplishment in the spiritual realm.

I believe that everyone has broken a fast at least once or twice in their lives. I have even been the victim of breaking fasts with some of the situations mentioned in the previous topic. While breaking a fast early should not be taken lightly, you should also not allow the devil to discourage you from fasting in the future. If you break a fast, the following guidelines may help you.

1. Ask For Forgiveness

When you break a fast, what you have done is broken your commitment to the Lord. Therefore, you should pray and ask the Lord to forgive you for breaking your fast and thereby breaking your commitment to Him.

God understands the struggles that we have in our flesh, and He understands the difficulty we experience in keeping our fast. So when you ask for forgiveness for breaking your fast, the Lord will forgive you. Do not allow condemnation to set upon your heart and discourage you from fasting. If you repent from your heart for breaking your fast, know in your heart that God has forgiven you.

2. Recommit Another Fast

If you give into temptation and break your fast before time, recommit another fast and get back in the fight. Many people break their fast and allow condemnation and discouragement to stop them from fasting. Never allow the devil to get the victory over you. Don't allow your shortcomings to stop you. Get back in the battle and continue the fight until you get the victory.

> *For a just man falleth seven times, and riseth up again...*
>
> *Proverbs 24:16*

This passage shows us the same thing we are saying above. There may be shortcomings in your life, but if you can rise up again, you can get the victory. In a war, many battles and skirmishes fought. Because you lose a battle or a scrimmage does not mean that you lose the war. In World Wars I and II, America lost many battles and scrimmages but we won the war. Likewise, in our spiritual warfare there will be many battles that are lost, but you will still win the war.

> *And he spake a parable unto them to this end, that men ought always to pray, and not to faint; Saying, There was in a city a judge, which feared not God, neither regarded man: And there was a widow in that city; and she came unto him, saying, Avenge me of mine adversary. And he would not for a while: but afterward he said within himself, Though I fear not God, nor regard man; Yet because this widow troubleth me, I will avenge her, lest by her continual coming she weary me.*
>
> *Luke 18:1-5*

In this passage, this widow received her justice because she was persistent. She continued to come over and over again until she received what she had requested. If you break a fast, commit another fast unto the Lord. You can start the fast the next day if you like, or even immediately after you have broken your fast. However, you may want to go on a lesser type of fast if you continually fail to complete your fast.

The key is to get back in the fight by getting back on your fast. By recommitting your fast you are saying to the devil that you still have the victory and that he will not triumph over you.

3. Try Focusing More on Spiritual Things

If you repeatedly break your fast, you may need to become more focused on the things of God. When I say, "more focused," I'm talking about reading, praying and confessing the Word of God, and filling your mind with other spiritual things while you are fasting.

Some people find everything in the world to do while they are on their fast simply to help them pass the time. The key to fasting is not simply to do without food for a period of time; it is to also focus your attention upon the Lord and allow your spirit to become more sensitive to Him. If you would begin to focus on spiritual things, it will help you to strengthen your spiritual muscles and help give you the mind, will, and endurance you need to complete your fast and achieve your victory.

4. Try Going On A Lesser Fast

If you continually break your fasts, it may mean that you need to reassess what type of fast you are attempting. We gave an example earlier about how a weight lifter must gradually work their way up to a substantial amount of weight. If a person was to go into a gym and attempt to lift 200 pounds for the first time, that amount might be overwhelming for that person. But if they started with 50 pounds and gradually increased the weight by 10 or 15 pounds over a period of time they would eventually be able to lift 200 pounds.

The type of fast you are attempting could be the equivalent of the weight lifter lifting too much weight for the first time. You may need to just start with a partial fast or another type of fast for a half a day. This may not seem like much of a challenge, but if you can consistently finish a short, easy fast, it will give you the confidence and faith you need to also accomplish a more difficult and lengthy fast. After successfully completing some of the easier fasts, you will eventually be able to build yourself up to the point where you can finish even difficult fasts in victory.

Chapter 12

How to Properly End Your Fast

I remember when I was a young Christian going on a three-day absolute fast. I remember the fast ending Friday evening at 6:00 p.m. I started the fast Tuesday evening at the same time and was now just about finished with my fast. As the seconds ticked off the clock towards 6:00, at 5:59 I was sitting outside Burger King waiting for my fast time to end. When it ended, I went in and ordered a double beef whopper, an extra-large fry, a giant fish sandwich, and an extra large cola. In my mind, I had not eaten in three days and I needed to at least eat enough food for one of the three days I had missed.

After finishing this fast-food-feast, my stomach began to cramp and ache me something terrible. The stomach pains and stomach gas made my evening and night very miserable. I quickly learned that this was not the way to come off of a fast.

If you have been on an absolute, normal or juice fast for two or more days, you should come off of it slowly. Whenever you go on a long fast, your stomach will go through a type of shrinking process. This is one of the reasons why your stomach will cramp if you overindulge in your first meal when you break your fast.

If you have fasted for an extended length of time (three or more days), it is recommended that you come off your fast with soft liquids such as soup or other types of soft foods for the first day. Since you have been fasting, the temptation will be there to overindulge, but you must resist the temptation to overindulge and eat sensibly. If you do not, you may pay for it (like I did) with stomachaches and pains. The next day you can eat more solid foods. By the third day, you should be able to eat normally.

Don't Allow Your Flesh to Go Wild

After your fast has ended, you will experience a heightened sense of spirituality, a heightened sense of sensitivity to the Holy Spirit, and a deeper intimacy with the Lord. This is definitely not the place that Satan wants you to remain in. He will therefore immediately attempt to get you away from that state and back to a carnal state as quickly as he can.

Just as you will be tempted to overindulge in food because you have abstained from eating the past few days, Satan will also tempt you to overindulge in other carnal things. But just as you cannot allow your flesh to overindulge in food, you must also resist the temptation to overindulge in carnal things such as watching too much (or the wrong kind of) television, movies or other things that may draw your heart away from God. When you finish your fast and finally allow your flesh to enjoy some pleasures and entertainment, it will want to act like a child in a toy store. It will want to go wild.

Some people come off a fast, and because they let the flesh loose, it gets out of control. Satan uses this spiritual liberty and spiritual letdown to catch them off guard and get them involved in things that hurt them spiritually. Many end up undermining (the spirit) in a day, or sometimes in only a few hours or even minutes, what they had worked hard during the time of their fast to accomplish or gain.

When Jesus fasted 40 days in the wilderness, it wasn't until after His fast had ended that the devil confronted Him with the temptations. I have always wondered why Satan waited until Jesus had finished His fast before attacking Him with a barrage of temptations. It would seem to me that the best time to try Him would have been before He began His fast, or at the beginning of His fast. But the Lord showed me that one of the reasons why the temptation came afterwards was because Satan knows the propensity that people sometimes have of relaxing and letting their guards down after finishing a fast.

He was attempting to catch Jesus off guard—hoping that he could catch Jesus in a vulnerable state while His flesh was hungering for carnal things. But thank God that Satan failed, and Jesus remained victorious.

Satan will likewise attempt to catch you off your guard when you finish your fast. But don't allow the kid (your soul) loose in the toy store. Put some restraints on your child (your soul). Yes, you can now enjoy some television, movies, music, games, and other forms of entertainment and pleasure, but don't allow Satan to get you out of control. If you can retain some discipline with your flesh and soul after finishing a victorious fast, you have just graduated and come up another level in Christ.

Before You Eat

Before eating your first meal, consummate your fast with prayer. Spend a few minutes thanking God for giving you the strength, mind and will to complete your fast. Give Him thanksgiving for what you have accomplished through your fast, not only in the physical realm, but also in the spiritual realm. Declare Satan's defeat in your life. Declare your triumph over whatever it is you have been fasting for, and decree your victory. After you have finished, spend a few moments worshiping and praising God for what He has done. And, now, you are finally ready to eat.

Other Books and Materials
By Kenneth Scott

The Weapons Of Our Warfare, Volume 1

The Weapons Of Our Warfare, Volume 2

The Weapons Of Our Warfare, Volume 3
—Confessing God's Word Over Your Life.

Volume 3, Confessions on CD and Cassette

The Weapons Of Our Warfare, Volume 4
—Prayers for Teenagers and Young Adults

The Weapons Of Our Warfare Prayers
on Audio Cassette Tapes

When All Hell Breaks Loose

Understanding Your Divine Authority In Prayer

Understanding The Lord's Prayer
—The Basics of Prayer

Standing In The Gap

Decreeing your Healing — Mini-booklet

Cassette Taped Messages

For other available materials, visit us on the web at:

www.spiritualwarfare.cc

Contact Us:

For prayer requests, questions or comments, write to:

Spiritual Warfare Ministries
Attention: Kenneth Scott
P.O. Box 2024
Birmingham, Alabama 35201-2024

(205) 853-9509

Web Site: www.spiritualwarfare.cc
email us at sprwarfare@aol.com

This book is not available in all bookstores. To order copies of this book, please send $8.99 plus $1.90 shipping and handling to the above address.

God has anointed Pastor Scott to teach and preach on the power of prayer. If you are interested in him coming to minister at your church or organization, please contact him at the information above.